THE CIVIL RIGHTS
MOVEMENT
AND ITS LEGACY

THE CIVIL
RIGHTS
MOVEMENT
AND
ITS LEGACY

BY ANNA KOSOF

Franklin Watts · 1989
New York · London · Toronto · Sydney

Photographs courtesy of
UPI/Bettmann: pp. 24, 27, 32, 35, 39, 43, 47, 48,
51, 53, 55 (both), 57, 65, 67, 77, 84 (both), 94;
Gamma/Liaison: p. 86 (Yvonne Hemsey).

Library of Congress Cataloging-in-Publication Data

Kosof, Anna.
The civil rights movement and its legacy / Anna Kosof.
p.   cm.
Bibliography: p.
Includes index.
Summary: Discusses the civil rights movement in America and its
effects on current society.
ISBN 0-531-10791-4
1. Afro-Americans—Civil rights.   2. Civil rights movements—
United States—History—20th century.   3. Minorities—United
States—Social conditions.   4. United States—Social
conditions—1945–   [1. Civil rights movements. 2. Afro-Americans—
Civil rights.]   I. Title.
E185.61.K62   1989
323.1'196073—dc20   89-9166 CIP AC

ACKNOWLEDGMENTS

During the years 1968 and 1969, as producer of a radio talk show, "Night Line," I conducted hundreds of hours of taped interviews with people who were active in the civil rights movement. Twenty years later many of my impressions and conclusions gleaned from these interviews have helped to shape this book. In addition I found an invaluable resource in the film documentary *Eyes on the Prize* together with the book of the same title.

At the height of the movement I came to know many of those committed to it, to participate with them in some of the marches, and to be a part of that large crowd of people who stood in the shadow of the Lincoln Memorial to hear Dr. Martin Luther King, Jr., deliver his "I Have a Dream" speech at the culmination of the March on Washington.

To all those people who shared with me their hopes and aspirations during and after those turbulent years, I am most grateful.

*Dedicated to those who
sacrificed their lives*

CONTENTS

THE CIVIL RIGHTS
MOVEMENT
AND ITS LEGACY

INTRODUCTION

Where does the story of the civil rights movement begin? One could argue that it began with the abolitionists of the early 1800s who fought to do away with the institution of slavery on the grounds that it was inhumane and unjust. One could say that it began with the Emancipation Proclamation, issued by President Abraham Lincoln during the Civil War (1861–1865).

With the war's end thousands of slaves became free men and women. The Emancipation Proclamation, however, had not spelled out just how these newly freed people were to be treated. This issue—how to treat ex-slaves—has been the center of turmoil ever since.

In 1896 the "separate but equal" doctrine was established in the case of *Plessy* v. *Ferguson*. The plaintiff, Homer Plessy, having purchased a train ticket from New Orleans to Covington, Louisiana, sat in a car reserved for whites only, refusing to sit in the section reserved for "coloreds." The police dragged him off the train and arrested him. He sued the railroad, contending that under the Fourteenth Amendment, ratified in 1868, ensuring equal protection for newly freed slaves, segregation was illegal.

Eventually the case was argued before the Supreme Court which ruled against him. The Court's decision, based on the Civil Rights Act of 1875, stated only that the law guaranteed all Americans the right to public accommodations—it said nothing about segregation. "Separate but equal" was all that was required by law. Therefore, *Plessy* v. *Ferguson* gave legal validity to segregation. Later numerous attempts were made to overturn the decision, opponents arguing that "separate but equal" is by definition not equality. Not until 1954, with the *Brown* decision, did a significant change come about.

Therefore, while one could begin the story of the civil rights movement in the eighteenth century, most people would agree that the present civil rights movement began on May 17, 1954, when the Supreme Court handed down the *Brown* v. *Board of Education of Topeka* decision, prohibiting segregation in public schools. It is at this historic point that we will begin our examination of the civil rights movement and its impact.

· · · · ·

For those who did not live through it, the civil rights movement is almost impossible to imagine. In every sense of the word, the struggle to make *Brown* v. *Board of Education* a reality was the beginning of a true revolution—by desegregating a society that was accustomed to seeing "whites only" signs everywhere. This was a society in which blacks customarily had to sit at the back of the bus, where elderly black people had to give up their seat for young white children, where black maids could enter their place of employment only through the back door (yet had sole charge of raising and caring for white children); in this society blacks and whites could not drink from the same water fountain, could not attend the same schools or churches.

This revolution to desegregate society took hundreds of lives; thousands of people were brutally beaten; churches and homes were firebombed. Thousands marched in protest; hundreds of others took part in boycotts against restaurants, buses, and stores. Nightly on television news those removed from the strife saw the National Guard protecting black students trying to integrate Southern schools. Viewers watched police dogs attack children, and Southern policemen use high-powered fire hoses and billy clubs to disperse demonstrators who were nonviolently exercising their right to assemble.

It may be hard to imagine that high school students were an integral part of that movement, but they were. At a very young age they confronted hatred and brutality, and some died. The movement had an immense impact on all who participated in it.

· · · · ·

The civil rights movement also profoundly affected the rest of society. It changed not only the way we saw others, but how we saw ourselves. Out of the fight for civil rights came the women's movement and the gay rights movement. Advocates for the disabled, for the disenfranchised (such as American Indians and Hispanic farm workers), and for the elderly have also followed the path blazed by those in the civil rights movement. And while some issues are unique to a specific advocacy, a common principle is shared by all—equality, in terms of employment, housing, access to education, and all those aspects of life that white males had taken for granted for so long.

In a short period of thirty years, we have moved from a country where people were killed for exercising their constitutional right to vote to a land where, in 1988, the Reverend Jesse Jackson was the runner-up for the Democratic presidential candidacy, triumphing over six white candidates and capturing twice as many white votes as he did in 1984 (when he ran for the same office).

· · · · ·

Although much progress has been made, we still have a long way to go. On the plus side for the first time in history there are twenty-three members of Congress who are black. But still, while blacks make up 11 percent of the voting age population, only 1.3 percent of the nation's five hundred thousand elected officials are black.[1]

In 1968 the Kerner Commission, which had been appointed by President Lyndon Johnson to study race relations, concluded, "We are moving toward two separate societies, one black and one white—separate and unequal." According to Vernon Jordan, the former president of the National Urban League, a major civil rights organization, "In 1988 that prophecy still rings true."[2]

The sociologist William Julius Wilson points out that in the ten largest cities in the United States the number of blacks living in extreme poverty increased 104 percent between 1970 and 1980. Furthermore, the number of Hispanics in extreme poverty increased threefold. The number of households headed by single women is at an all-time high, resulting in a record number of women and children living in poverty, with a significant number of them homeless.[3]

Today, 71 percent of black citizens feel that prejudice still remains an obstacle to them. "It's subtle racism, but lethal. It wears you down," says Dr. Alvin Poussaint, professor of psychiatry at Harvard University.

The police and the dogs are missing, federal marshals no longer have to protect Southern black students at school, yet there is a growing number of racial incidents taking place. Some of the neo-Nazi groups are again on the rise.

It's time to step back and assess our progress. How much have we really changed? Can we say that we are now a society that treats all people equally, regardless of color or creed? Can we say that thirty-five years after the *Brown* decision we now live in a "color-blind" society where all people have equal access to good housing, education, and employment? This book is a journey through the years of struggle for equality, and how it touched us all. The civil rights movement was a revolutionary philosophy whose effects continue to reverberate today.

1

THE IMPACT OF
BROWN V.
BOARD OF EDUCATION

The Reverend Martin Luther King, Jr., and the Reverend Jesse Jackson are the best-known soldiers of the civil rights movement. But the fact that they were able to accomplish so much is due in large part to the efforts of those who came before—men and women like W. E. B. DuBois, Mary Church Terrell, Charles Houston, and Thurgood Marshall.

Indeed, Houston and Marshall fought long and hard in the courts, tackling countless cases involving segregation. Out of their dedication came the Legal Defense Fund, a special division of the NAACP (National Association for the Advancement of Colored People), set up in 1946 by Marshall when he became the new special counsel for the organization. At that time Houston and Marshall were still challenging the "separate but equal" Plessy doctrine. But with the end of World War II, some things had changed.

For the first time in history, thousands of black Americans had fought in a world war. They had fought for democracy and against the excesses of the Nazis and the Japanese. They had fought in segregated units and on foreign soil. Yet, those who survived the war returned home to a country where "separate but equal" was still the law.

How could a country expect to send soldiers abroad to defend it, yet not entitle them to equality on their own soil? Certainly, a new way of thinking had to evolve.

· · · · ·

Charles Houston was in the hospital in early 1950 after having suffered a heart attack when a case of major concern to him, the *Consolidated Parents Group* case, came before the U.S. Supreme Court.

The Consolidated Parents Group was a Washington, D.C., organization of black parents who brought suit against the city, protesting the over-crowded all-black school that was built to accommodate eight hundred and actually had eighteen hundred in attendance, while a nearby all-white school was half empty.

For years Houston had represented the group, fighting the case through the courts, but now, just as it had reached the highest court in the land, he was forced to turn the case over to a colleague and friend, James M. Nabrit, Jr., the future president of Howard University.

In preparing to argue the case before the Supreme Court, Nabrit decided to change tactics. Instead of fighting the case on the grounds that black schools should be equal to those available to whites, Nabrit proposed that the Legal Defense Fund challenge the very concept of racial segregation in the school system.

This change in tactics may not seem all that significant at first glance, but it was to have a major impact. It is one thing to argue that blacks should have schools as good as those for whites, but quite another to dispute the entire notion that blacks should be segregated. Many people were agreeable to an "equal" education for blacks as long as they were separated from whites, but now the very idea that something could be both separate and equal was being challenged.

Nabrit recalls saying to Charles Houston, "If I take these cases, I am telling you now I am going to abandon this separate-but-equal theory you have, and I am going to draft a new theory. I am going to try these cases on the theory that segregation per se is unconstitutional."[1] According to Nabrit, Houston (who died a short time later) came to see things the same way.

One of the first major breakthroughs came in 1950. Herman Sweatt, a black, had applied to the law school at the University of Texas in Austin. The school accepted him but offered a special arrangement. A special classroom would be set up in the basement of the school, and there he would be taught by part-time faculty members. The NAACP brought suit, arguing that this offer was hardly equal to what was offered to white students.

A lower court ruling against Sweatt resulted in a long legal battle. Eventually, the case reached the Supreme Court, and on June 5, 1950, the Court handed down a carefully crafted decision. In effect the justices said that "separate but equal" education was not just a meaningless phrase, that it had to be genuine, or the separation was indeed unconstitutional.

While the Supreme Court still had not struck down the *Plessy* decision, the NAACP and its legal arm, the Legal Defense Fund, had come close to achieving their goal. The major thrust of their battle was to show that separate schools could never be equal. They had to demonstrate the harmful effects of segregation, including the psychological and financial. They knew that in order to do so, they would need to broaden their scope, so they compiled individual cases from different states, with different situations.

In preparing their argument, they enlisted the help of Dr. Kenneth Clark, a well-known psychologist who had demonstrated in a creative way the effects that segregation had on children. Giving both black and white dolls to young black children, he asked them questions about the different dolls. The results were startling. Most of the children saw themselves as inferior. Most of them saw the black dolls as "bad" and the white dolls as "nice." Dr. Clark said in an interview, "Segregation was, is, the way in which society tells a group of human beings that they are inferior to other groups of human beings in the society. . . . It influences the child's view of himself."[2]

Dr. Clark's argument of psychologically based findings did not change the law. In fact, in one of the many different cases that the Legal Defense Fund presented to the Court, this argument proved futile. The federal court found Dr. Clark's point irrelevant.

While the Legal Defense Fund had made some progress in its arguments before the Court, it still had a long way to go. Soon the battleground would shift to a school system in the Midwest.

. . . . .

Linda Brown lived in Topeka, Kansas. As a seven-year-old black child, she had to cross railroad tracks every day to wait for a rundown bus to take her to a black school, even though there was another school, all white, closer to her home. When her parents sued the board of education, the judge in the case dismissed the plaintiff's arguments, ruling that the Topeka board of education had broken no law.

The NAACP decided that the case was worth carrying all the way to the Supreme Court, and in 1952, the Court, under Chief Justice Frederick Vinson, agreed to hear *Brown* v. *Board of Education.*

Many times in the past the NAACP had come close to overturning segregation, but the lower courts still upheld segregation in some form. In one case the court argued that separate schools resulted not from racism but from Southern "mores."

The Supreme Court deliberations went on for months. After nearly a year no decision had been handed down. Then in September 1953, Chief Justice Vinson died, and Earl Warren was appointed by President Dwight Eisenhower to fill the vacancy. This man was new to most of the NAACP staff, causing them considerable anxiety. No one really knew where Warren stood on the civil rights question, and yet it would be under his leadership that this significant issue would be decided.

On May 17, 1954, Chief Justice Warren read the Supreme Court's first major ruling since he assumed office. In delivering the court's decision, he said, "We conclude, unanimously, that in the field of public education the doctrine of 'separate but equal' has no place. Separate educational facilities are inherently unequal."

The Court's ruling marked the end of an era. Southern politicians almost unanimously denounced the decision. Extremists warned that it would result in intermarriages and would destroy the separation of the races. Major newspapers across the country called the decision a landmark that would alter the very fabric of American life. To blacks, it offered the promise of better times to come. But they also knew that the law was one thing and action was still another matter.

Thurgood Marshall, today a Supreme Court justice, was one of the many lawyers who argued the *Brown* case. Later, looking back on the case, Marshall credited Charles Houston, a man little known outside the civil rights movement, as the architect of it all. He had won the most important civil rights case of the twentieth century.

But the jubilation did not last long. On May 17, 1954, "Black Monday," Mississippi Senator James Eastland declared, "You are not obliged to obey the decisions of any court which are plainly fraudulent sociological considerations."[3] While the Court handed down a clear decision for integration of the schools, it did not provide any instructions as to how this was to be carried out. Most of the nation waited and did nothing to change its school systems, while the more militant segregationists clamored for the impeachment of Chief Justice Warren.

President Eisenhower in no way aligned himself with the decision. While 1954 marked the end of an era, in many ways it also marked the beginning of the next major struggle—the implementation of the Supreme Court ruling.

Lawyers who argued the case against segregation stand in front of the U.S. Supreme Court building on May 17, 1954, after the high tribunal ruled that segregation is unconstitutional. Left to right are: George E. C. Hayes, Thurgood Marshall, and James M. Nabrit, Jr.

Looking back at the 1950s now, it is hard to overestimate the suffering and pain that this decision inflicted on black citizens. It was a time of hatred and violence—and murder; it was also a time of enormous hope and determination to bring about change. While racially motivated murders were not new to the South, in 1955 several blacks were killed, two of whom were NAACP organizers trying to register people to vote.

· · · · ·

Emmett Till was an unlikely hero, a fourteen-year-old boy who in 1955 sparked history and became one of the symbols of the violence that segregationists were capable of committing.

Emmett was from Chicago, visiting relatives in Mississippi. Emmett thought that he knew the unwritten rules of segregation, but he did not understand the Southern type of segregation. His family tried to coach him in how to behave around white folks. Apparently he did not take their advice.

One day, according to his cousin, Curtis Jones, he, Emmett, and some friends went into the local white-owned grocery store, where Emmett flirted with a white woman. Upon leaving, he was heard to say "Bye, Baby." At that point all the boys ran away.

But the story doesn't end there. The next day, when the woman's husband returned from a trip, he and his friends came to look for Emmett at his uncle's house, where he had been staying. They threatened his uncle, Morris Wright, with death, and dragged the fourteen-year-old into the back of the car and drove away.

Emmett Till's body was found later. He had been shot in the head, and his forehead had been crushed. His body was so mutilated that it was hard to identify him.

His assailants were indicted for his murder, but at the trial Emmett's cousin Curtis was forbidden by his mother to testify, because, in the atmosphere of the times, blacks dared not testify against a white. They feared the consequences.

But Morris Wright, Emmett's uncle, agreed to be a witness. Michigan congressman Charles Diggs later recalled, "It was the first time in the history of Mississippi that a Negro had stood in court and pointed his finger at a white man as a killer of a Negro."[4]

Medgar Evers, an NAACP organizer later murdered, took Wright out of the state for safety after he testified.

The case attracted a lot of interest. Even some of the most conservative Southerners were shocked about the brutality of the murder of a fourteen-year-old. Some likened the case to that of Anne Frank, a Jewish girl killed by the Nazis. However, although the two men who dragged Emmett Till away were clearly identified, the jury reached a verdict of "not guilty."

Black Americans were outraged. How could the justice system let the murderers go free, sanctioning the killing of a child whose "crime" was saying "Bye, Baby" to a white woman? On the one hand, according to the Supreme Court, blacks were entitled to equal education, but in defiance of the law—as Emmett Till's murder proved—blacks were not treated equally. The greatest challenge then was to put the law into practice. If separate was not equal, then all the established institutions had to be challenged.

Pictured here in court with their children, defendants
John Milam and Roy Bryant were tried in Sumner,
Mississippi, for the "Wolf-Whistle" murder of fourteen-
year-old Emmett Till. The granduncle of the victim
identified Milam and Bryant as the two men who
spirited Till away on the night of August 28, 1955.

Why should blacks have to ride in the back of the bus if they were equal to whites? Why couldn't they drink from the same water fountain or eat at the same lunch counter? And what about their right to vote, to be full citizens, a right guaranteed by the Constitution? Each of these issues became a struggle in itself, and each victory led to another battle.

Perhaps at no other time in our history, with the exception of the Civil War, did such hatred and resistance to change manifest itself as in the years that followed. Nor had there ever been such single-minded determination by blacks to see that change did occur.

2

CHALLENGING DAILY HUMILITATION: MONTGOMERY AND LITTLE ROCK

Today when we read about apartheid in South Africa, many of us think about it as something outside our ken, but the American South before 1960 was not much different. The same enforced separation of the races existed.

Perhaps one of the most degrading experiences that blacks confronted daily was that, when they rode on public buses, they were required to sit in the back. Only whites were allowed to sit in the front of the bus. In some cities black people had to pay their fare to the driver in the front, then disembark and reenter through the rear door. As the bus became more crowded with white passengers, blacks would be ordered to give up their seats. Or even when the front of the bus was empty—as was often the case in Montgomery, Alabama, where black riders accounted for over 75 percent of the riders—they still had to go to the back and stand.

This "separate" practice was first challenged in Baton Rouge, Louisiana, in 1953, where blacks won the right of first-come, first-seated. They were still separated—blacks in the back, whites in the front—but blacks no longer had to surrender their seats to whites if there were no more seats in the front. This may not have seemed to be much of a victory, but the news spread quickly to other places where blacks were ready to fight the same battle against forced segregation on buses.

It was in Montgomery, Alabama, however, that a major victory was achieved.

· · · · ·

When black leaders decided to organize a bus boycott in Montgomery, the 1954 Supreme Court decision on school desegregation was vivid in the minds of some of them. If the court would rule that school segregation was unconstitutional, then what about another public system—buses? Just as *Brown v. Board of Education* was an attempt to end school segregation, the Montgomery boycott was an attempt to desegregate public transportation.

The Montgomery bus boycott is a story of immense courage. Those who took part in it risked being fired from their jobs, or harassed, or, worse, beaten. It is also the story of a major organizational effort. The NAACP organizers of the boycott knew that to get forty-five thousand blacks to boycott the buses was a monumental task. Yet they also knew that this was the only way the boycott would succeed.

Claudette Colvin, a black teenager, could easily have become as well known as Rosa Parks. In 1955 she was dragged off a city bus and arrested because she refused to give up her seat on the bus when told to do so by the driver. When she was found guilty of assault, her lawyer prepared to appeal the case on the grounds that segregated seating on public transportation was unconstitutional, but just as her case was about to go to federal court, she became pregnant.

Given the temper of the times, when pregnancy out of wedlock was condemned, the NAACP decided to look elsewhere for someone to serve as a test case, someone whose character was above reproach. In December 1955 they found their person in Rosa Parks, a soft-spoken forty-three-year-old seamstress who was active in the church and served as secretary for the local chapter of the NAACP.

Fifteen years earlier she had also experienced the humiliation of being dragged off a bus for refusing to give up her seat. This time, when Mrs. Parks refused to surrender her seat at the bus driver's request, she was arrested, tried, and found guilty of violating the law banning integration.

Upon her conviction, leaders in the black community, seeing that this was their opportunity to challenge segregation in public transportation, formed the Montgomery Improvement Association. Leading the protest group was the new pastor of the Dexter Avenue Baptist Church. He was twenty-six years old and had recently completed his studies in theology at Boston College. His name was Martin Luther King, Jr.

Jo Ann Robinson, one of the organizers of the protest, recalls working through the night mimeographing thousands of leaflets for distribution throughout the black community. The flier told of Mrs. Parks's arrest and urged people to protest in an effective but nonviolent way: "Don't ride the

Mrs. Rosa Parks, whose arrest in December 1955 sparked the boycott of Montgomery blacks against the city's bus lines, sits in the front of a city bus shortly after a Supreme Court ruling outlawed segregation on the city's public transit vehicles.

bus to work, to town, to school, or any place Monday. . . ."[1]

The word was out. The local newspaper carried the story of the impending boycott on the front page.

On that famous Monday Mrs. Parks was found guilty of violating the laws of segregation and was fined ten dollars plus court fees.

The same day, the buses were all but empty as black workers found other means of transportation. Black-owned taxis were enlisted to take people to and from work, for the same fare as the passengers would have had to pay on the bus—ten cents. Those who owned their own cars also helped transport people to and from work. And some people walked.

· · · · ·

Clearly, this one-day boycott showed that blacks were willing to stand united. Now the question was whether the boycott should and could continue. The black preachers, with their new leader, met to decide what to do next. They decided to continue.

The protesters' demands were modest. They asked that seating on city buses be on a first-come, first-seated basis, even though blacks would still sit in the back of the bus; that they be treated courteously; and that blacks be hired as drivers on all-black routes. The city commissioners, however, would agree to none of their demands. And further, they implied their belief that by giving in to the protesters, they would just be subjected to more and more demands.

As the boycott continued, whites joined in the protest. Many white women who employed black women as domestics helped transport them back and forth to work. The Jewish community raised money to support the boycott, and as the news reached the North, Northern sympathizers raised funds too.

No amount of pressure to end the boycott dampened the determination of the protesters. The weeks turned into months, and then into a year.

Eventually the economic effects on the white community began to be felt—by the bus company, which had lost the daily fares of its black passengers, and by the downtown business frequented by blacks, who could not get downtown because of the boycott. Blacks in Montgomery for the first time demonstrated their unity and determination and, most importantly, their power.

The black community paid a price, however—not only in tired and sore feet, but in more frightening matters. The homes of many of the organizers, including Dr. King's home and that of one of his closest aides, Dr. Ralph Abernathy, were bombed. A grand jury indicted nearly one hundred blacks—Dr. King and dozens of other ministers among them—for conspiracy to boycott. They were tried and found guilty. Dr. King was fined five hundred dollars and sentenced to over a year of hard labor. With Dr. King's indictment, the story of the Montgomery boycott reached the front page of the nation's newspapers.

Nearly a year later, after a year of hardship for the black community, after homes were fire-bombed, and insurance coverages for the organizing churches were revoked, the Supreme Court affirmed a lower court decision outlawing segre-

The Reverend Martin Luther King, Jr., and his wife (center) smile broadly in front of a group of supporters following King's conviction for his part in the Montgomery bus boycott.

gation on buses. After a year, thousands of blacks resumed riding the Montgomery City Lines buses.

· · · · ·

The boycott brought many things—increased anger and violence from staunch segregationists, but an enormous new sense of pride and victory for blacks. Many people who lived through that era never thought that the day would come when they could not be ordered to the back of the bus, but now blacks could by law ride buses with whites on an equal basis. There was also a new organization, the Southern Christian Leadership Conference, an association of churches and civic groups, headed by the young pastor, Reverend Dr. Martin Luther King, Jr.

· · · · ·

But after their victory in Montgomery, blacks found themselves facing the reality of white intransigence. In the wake of the Supreme Court's decision that segregation was unlawful, only two Southern states took action to bring about desegregation. Getting municipalities to abide by the law was the next great challenge, and a most unlikely place, Little Rock, Arkansas, became the battleground.

In 1957, the Little Rock school board was the first in the South to issue a statement to the effect that they would comply with the Supreme Court decision. It seemed that here desegregation would be a smooth and easy process. The board moved ahead to develop a plan, known as the Little Rock Phase Program, under which one school, Central

High, would admit a limited number of black students. The board argued that they were not delaying desegregation but rather wanted a gradual approach. The Supreme Court, however, ruled that desegregation should be implemented with "deliberate speed."

While whites opposed the Phase Program, Thurgood Marshall and other NAACP lawyers saw that this gradual and limiting program had to be challenged. They took the case to court. This move further angered some whites, who felt that they were moving with speed and that they were genuinely trying to desegregate the school system.

It was in Little Rock that the battle turned one American against another, and the young people bore the brunt of the struggle. No longer were the battles for desegregation fought in prestigious courts. Now the battleground was Central High School.

It was also in Little Rock that desegregation became a political football, as the reelection of politicians became dependent on taking a strong stand for segregation.

Arkansas Governor Orval Faubus, who was not known to be solidly for segregation, saw that in order to be reelected, he had to at least publicly deliver strong statements supporting his most segregationist constituency.

Not surprisingly, only a few black students had enrolled at Central High. Intimidated by threats and anonymous phone calls, most of the black children eligible to attend chose not to, but nine took their place in history.

As time grew closer for those nine black children, out of a student body of two thousand, to enter Central High, Governor Faubus issued a statement that National Guardsmen would be stationed at the school to maintain order. He asked that black students not attend any white schools in the city until the situation was resolved.

The situation grew ugly. On the opening day of the school year, one black student who had not heard about Governor Faubus's request, Elizabeth Eckford, fifteen years old, got off the bus and walked through an angry mob of whites who shouted epithets and threatened to lynch her. A white parent saved her and got her back home before any physical harm could be done to her.

In the meantime, as the governor kept the black students from enrolling in school, the Justice Department ruled that there was no evidence that violence would erupt if blacks were allowed to attend Central High. But Faubus continued to station the National Guardsmen at the school to keep black students from attending.

As the threat of violence spread, the governor was summoned to meet with President Eisenhower. Although Eisenhower was not a strong supporter of desegregation, he held strongly to the belief that all people must obey the law, and he sought to

An angry student (center background) shouts epithets at Elizabeth Eckford (foreground) as she tries to gain entrance to Little Rock's Central High School. The battle to desegregate the Arkansas school marked the first great confrontation between the South and the federal government over civil rights.

persuade Faubus to take a determined stand to integrate the schools.

As the situation became more and more volatile, the parents of the black students asked for federal protection for their children. President Eisenhower responded by sending riot-trained units of the 101st Airborne Division to Little Rock. For the first time Americans watched televised newscasts of federal troops protecting black children, and later, in a nationally televised address, Eisenhower made it clear that he would defend the law and not permit its obstruction.

The sight of federal troops protecting black children against white citizens made an indelible impression on all who witnessed it. Many of those in the black community felt that they really were American citizens at last. But most whites responded with anger to what they believed was the federal government's interference in local matters.

Ernest Green was the only black to graduate from Central High the first year. He became a symbol of what that year was like for those nine students who attended school in spite of physical danger, harassment, and abuse, and who were daily escorted to and from school by federal troops. The following year the public schools were closed. Most of the white students went to private schools or did not attend school at all. Again, the Supreme Court had to intervene, ruling that closing the public school was unconstitutional and used to circumvent the law.

In Little Rock real battle lines were drawn, as black people risked not only their own lives but those of their children for the right to receive the same quality of education as white children did.

3

A NEW GENERATION
COMES OF AGE

In 1960 a new generation of blacks took their place on the front lines. These students, who were children in 1954, had lived through the beginning of the civil rights movement. Deeply influenced by *Brown* v. *Board of Education,* by the Montgomery bus boycott, by Little Rock, and by the hundreds of violent acts committed against blacks, they were ready to continue what others had begun. With this new generation and its awareness of the victories being won, a clear philosophy emerged—one of nonviolence.

It would have been a dream come true if the *Brown* decision had succeeded in overturning segregation, but this did not happen. Segregation had to be fought on a case-by-case basis, and each racist institution had to be attacked separately. The story of the great Montgomery victory achieved through nonviolence was told in a pamphlet titled "Martin Luther King and the Montgomery Story," thousands of copies of which were distributed by the Fellowship of Reconciliation (FOR).

James Lawson, a pacifist who had refused to fight in the Korean War during the 1950s, was one of the teachers of nonviolence. He was a theology student who had spent time with Mahatma Gandhi in India and studied the use of nonviolence as a tool against oppression.

Student advocates of nonviolent protest began to challenge segregation laws at lunch counters in the South. These black students were permitted to spend money in stores like Woolworth's but could not sit down and be served at the stores' lunch counters. They could not even get a drink of water. To challenge this practice, black students would sit at the lunch counters without being served until the store closed. From a few isolated protests, the movement spread to dozens of other cities. In the North, liberal sympathizers picketed stores like Woolworth's for refusing to serve blacks in the South.

Diane Nash, like many other college students at the time, was anxious to be a part of the struggle. As one of the organizers of the sit-ins in Nashville, Tennessee, she recalled, "The first sit-ins we had were really funny. The waitresses were nervous. They must have dropped two thousand dollars worth of dishes that day . . . we were sitting there trying not to laugh, at the same time we were scared to death."[1] In one day over two hundred students mobilized for sit-ins.

But nonviolence is not an easy, painless struggle. On the contrary. In Nashville a gang of white students attacked the students sitting at the counter, beating them senselessly and shouting

This F. W. Woolworth store in Greensboro, North Carolina, was the birthplace of the sit-in movement that challenged segregation at lunch counters. The photo shows a group of black college students staging a sit-down strike in February 1960.

epithets. Although those at the counter did not fight back, when the police came, it was the black students who were arrested not the whites. The Nashville black community, united behind the students, raised over fifty thousand dollars for their fines and court fees, a hefty sum for the black community. The arrests did not deter the students. They continued the sit-ins, and they continued to be beaten and arrested.

Again, as in the Montgomery bus boycotts, businesses suffered. Store owners were anxious for a settlement of the sit-ins so that business could go on. But as the sit-ins continued, the violence increased, and the home of attorney Z. Alexander Looby, who defended the students in court, was bombed.

The bombing galvanized the students, and with an even greater resolve, they marched to city hall, twenty-five hundred strong. As the television cameras followed the demonstrators to the steps of city hall, Mayor Ben West came forward to meet them. In a now famous confrontation, the student Diane Nash asked him point-blank if he believed that segregation was wrong. He answered yes, and the next day a local newspaper carried the dramatic headline, "Mayor Says Integrate Counters."[2] A day later, Dr. King arrived in Nashville to join in the celebration and to gain inspiration from the students. Three weeks later the lunch counters were desegregated.

· · · · ·

The sit-ins moved to Atlanta. In October 1960 Dr. King was arrested there and sentenced to jail. His arrest took a dramatic turn. This was a presidential election year. John F. Kennedy, the Democratic candidate, heard of King's arrest and called Dr. King's wife, Coretta Scott King, to lend his support. Soon after, his brother Robert called the local authorities, and King was freed. A new alliance had been formed. The following month Kennedy, with overwhelming black support, won the presidential election.

· · · · ·

By 1961 the stage was set for new confrontations. Major civil rights organizations were formed, new leadership emerged, and a new president was elected who had some relationship to the movement and to Dr. King. Almost predictably, Southern officials had to oppose segregation, and the federal government had to step in to protect the civil rights workers, but each step of the way resulted in brutal clashes.

CORE, the Congress of Racial Equality, an organization formed in 1947, tried to end segregation on the interstate buses and trains. In the 1940s their attempts failed. In 1961 they decided to try again.

The Freedom Riders, as this integrated group came to be called, took a bus trip from Washington, D.C., through the Deep South. They traveled in Greyhound and Trailway buses. Their strategy was clear. They would defy segregation by having whites sit in the back of the bus while blacks would sit up front, refusing to move. At rest stops blacks would try to use the whites-only restrooms and eat at the whites-only lunch counters. Clearly, as James

Farmer, former leader of CORE, recalled, "They wanted to create a crisis to get the federal government to step in."[3]

When the first bus arrived in Anniston, Alabama, its thirteen riders were stoned and a firebomb was thrown into the bus. In Birmingham, where the other buses headed, the Freedom Riders found no better welcome. Southern extremists waited for them to arrive, and then they attacked.

Eugene "Bull" Connor, Birmingham's police commissioner, became the most telling symbol of what the Freedom Riders had to endure. At two o'clock one morning, he herded some of the students into police cars and drove them across the state line, dumping them beside a highway in Nashville, Tennessee. He then stood by as the Freedom Riders were beaten unconscious by white racists and were left lying on the road.[4]

The violence against the Freedom Riders was international news just as President Kennedy was scheduled to meet in Vienna with the Soviet leader Nikita Khrushchev. The United States could ill afford such negative worldwide press coverage concerning the treatment of blacks. Kennedy asked the leaders of the Freedom Rides to discontinue them until after his meeting with Khrushchev, but they refused.[5]

President Kennedy and his brother Robert, now the attorney general, had little choice but to protect the Freedom Riders. During that summer of 1961 more than three hundred buses traveled to the Deep South in an effort to overcome segregation. These confrontations were some of the most brutal in the entire civil rights movement.

Passengers of a Greyhound bus, some of them members of the "Freedom Riders" group, watch the burning bus after it was set afire by a group of whites on May 14, 1961.

*Birmingham's notorious police commissioner,
Eugene "Bull" Connor (coatless), leads
officers during a mass arrest.*

In the Freedom Rides a coalition of blacks and
Northern whites was formed. They rode the buses
together and endured beatings together. The
Southern extremists, in turn, responded to the new
coalition with greater and greater violence. Even a
representative from the Justice Department was
brutally beaten.

Segregationists were fighting against change,
and their resolve to fight was as strong as that of
those organizing to defeat segregation. But no
number of beatings, no amount of violence seemed

to deter the Freedom Riders. They continued to forge ahead, even when martial law was declared in Alabama. By now the NAACP had been outlawed in the state, and a new organization had taken its place. It was called the Alabama Christian Movement for Human Rights, under the leadership of the Reverend Fred Shuttlesworth. Clearly, blacks would not stop short of fighting for integration on every level of American life. They had gone too far and fought too hard not to continue.

• • • • •

There was nothing very special about Albany, Georgia, that would indicate that it would become a major battleground in the civil rights movement. It was predominantly a farming town, with a population over 40 percent black. As in most other Southern towns, in spite of the *Brown* decision, the schools here remained segregated, and very few blacks had been allowed to register to vote.

On November 1, 1961, a ruling by the Interstate Commerce Commission backed the Supreme Court decision prohibiting segregation in interstate bus and train stations. During the same month, both NAACP and SNCC* workers decided to test the ruling by sitting in the white waiting room at the Albany bus terminal. They were promptly arrested.

The arrest of the protesters galvanized the black community and gave birth to the Albany Movement. They held their first mass meeting in a church. The Freedom Riders, black and white,

*SNCC (Student Nonviolent Coordinating Committee) was founded in the spring of 1960 at Shaw University in Raleigh, North Carolina.

arrived in Albany, Georgia, the following month. They met with a similar fate. They were arrested for trespassing at Albany's Central Railway Terminal.

The next day, the national press arrived to witness a major demonstration called by SNCC organizer James Forman, who led a march of black high school students to the train station. All the students were arrested and jailed.

In the months that followed, there were more arrests and increasingly brutal confrontations. Dr. King and Dr. Ralph Abernathy were arrested while kneeling on the steps of city hall asking the white city officials for a meeting. Both leaders chose to go to jail rather than pay bail.

The following year Albany saw a Montgomery-style bus boycott, while SNCC organizers were arrested for everything from trying to obtain a library card, to sitting at a lunch counter. That same year Dr. King returned to Albany to stand trial for marching without a permit.

The atmosphere in Albany had reached crisis proportions. When Marion King, wife of Slater King (one of the leaders of the Albany Movement), took food to friends in jail, a guard knocked her down and kicked her until she became unconscious. Pregnant, she miscarried.[6]

The events in Albany gave the NAACP and the ministers the opportunity to meet with Attorney General Robert Kennedy and to ask that the president address the civil rights crisis on national television.

If things were brutal in Albany, Georgia, greater brutality was to come. Some have said that Albany was the training ground for Birmingham.

In Birmingham, Alabama's largest city, the median income of blacks in 1961 was three thousand dollars, less than half the income of whites. The city became infamous for the Mother's Day attack on the Freedom Riders by white extremists while FBI agents stood passively by.

Two years later it was also the city in which nearly a thousand black students were arrested and jailed for demonstrating. "Bull" Connor, hoping to deter the demonstrators, brought out the city police dogs. Demonstrators were subjected to electric cat-

Demonstrators took refuge in a doorway as firemen unleashed their water hoses during a Birmingham riot that led to the arrest of two hundred blacks.

tle prods and high-pressure hoses, and police clubbed those who had fallen. In protest other black students stayed home from school.

That same year, Alabama Governor George Wallace made history as he stood in the doorway of the University of Alabama, blocking black students from registering. It was Wallace who proclaimed to a cheering crowd during his famous inauguration speech, "Segregation now! Segregation tomorrow! Segregation forever!" About the same time the Ku Klux Klan bombed four black churches. And in Oxford, Mississippi, when James Meredith, a black, tried to register at Ole Miss (the University of Mississippi), riots broke out, two people were killed, and hundreds were injured. Meredith had to be escorted into school by federal troops in the middle of the night to avoid the violent mob. And Dr. King's home was bombed—again.

Nineteen sixty-three marked the hundredth anniversary of the Emancipation Proclamation. But the situation for blacks was bleak. Black unemployment was twice that of whites, and blacks earned less than half the salary of whites. For nearly ten years white Americans had watched newscasts and read stories of blacks being beaten and attacked by dogs and of black churches and homes being bombed. Something had to be done. President Kennedy spoke to the nation on television:

The fires of frustration and discord are burning in the streets, in demonstrations and parades of protests which create tensions and threaten violence. We face, therefore, a moral crisis as a country and as a people. . . . I am therefore asking the Congress to enact legislation giving

*James Meredith tried to break the race
barrier at the all-white University of Mississippi.
His bid to register was turned down twice by
Mississippi Governor Barnett.*

all Americans the right to be served in facilities which are open to the public—hotels, restaurants, theaters, retail stores and similar establishments.[7]

President Kennedy delivered a new civil rights bill to Congress on June 19, 1963. Within the bill was a voting rights provision, for even though the Constitution guaranteed this right, blacks living in the rural areas and small towns of the South could not register to vote without fear of reprisals.

To demonstrate support for the bill, all the various civil rights organizations* joined together for a march on Washington on August 28. Over two hundred and fifty thousand people came to Washington to show support for what they knew would be the most important single legislative act in the history of the civil rights movement.

Nineteen fifty-four, with the historic Supreme Court *Brown* decision, was a milestone; a decade later, 1963, with the March on Washington, was a milestone of equal importance.

The march's themes were unity, racial harmony, and, most of all, support for the civil rights bill. Blacks reached out to white groups who would also take part in the gathering. People came from all walks of life and from all parts of the country. Over two thousand chartered buses brought participants to Washington. It was the single greatest coalition of civil rights organizations, churches, and labor unions that this country had ever seen.

*These included the NAACP, CORE, SNCC, SCLC, the Urban League, and the Brotherhood of Sleeping Car Porters.

Above: Placard-bearing demonstrators literally jam Constitution Avenue and (below) tens of thousands of spectators pack the area around the Washington Monument during the 1963 civil rights March on Washington.

The Kennedy Justice Department tried to get the march called off, but the movement was too strong, its participants too determined. In anticipation of violence, some units of the National Guard and Army were put on alert.

A. Philip Randolph, head of the Brotherhood of Sleeping Car Porters and the civil rights movement's elder statesman, started off the program with a moving speech. "Fellow Americans," he addressed the quarter-million people on the lawn of the Lincoln Memorial,

> *we are gathered here in the largest demonstration in the history of this nation. Let the nation and the world know the meaning of our numbers. We are not pressure groups, we are not an organization or a group of organizations, we are not a mob. We are the advance guard of a massive moral revolution for jobs and freedom.*[8]

The event was a tremendous success. There was not one untoward incident or disturbance during the entire March, an astonishing fact. As television crews recorded the event, the nation saw black and white people marching side by side, brought together for one cause.

· · · · ·

While it was inspiring to be a part of the March on Washington, those who participated were aware that the struggle was far from over. The achievement of equality was still far, far away. The glory of that day faded quickly. Only a few days after the celebrated March, an incident in Birmingham shocked the world. The Ku Klux Klan bombed the all-black Sixteenth Street Baptist Church, killing

A Birmingham police officer assesses the damage outside the Sixteenth Street Baptist Church, where a bomb explosion killed four blacks and left at least a dozen wounded.

four young girls who were attending Bible school. The same day, police killed a black youth in the street, and another black man was attacked and murdered by a white mob.

A few months later, on November 22, 1963, President Kennedy was assassinated. The nation fell into mourning.

When Lyndon Baines Johnson, the new president and a Southerner himself, spoke to Congress, he said:

> No memorial or eulogy could more eloquently honor President Kennedy's memory than the earliest possible passage of the civil rights bill for which he fought. [The new president continued,] We have talked for one hundred years or more. Yes, it is time now to write the next chapter— and to write it in the book of Law.[9]

Perhaps now history was on the side of justice. But 1964 would prove to be a very painful year. Although the struggle was still far from over, the battle lines were clearly drawn.

4

FROM SELMA
TO MONTGOMERY

It seemed hard to imagine that after the March on
Washington so much work still needed to be done.
It seems hard now to conceive that one hundred
years after passage of the Fifteenth Amendment to
the constitution, prohibiting discrimination in voting, only 1 percent of blacks in Selma, Alabama, for
example, were registered to vote. For blacks, voting
was a difficult task. First they were intimidated by
white officials, and, in order to register, they were
required to complete a lengthy questionnaire that
was irrelevant and against the law.

While the civil rights bill that was sent to
Congress addressed the evils of discrimination in
public accommodations, it did not specifically focus
on the right to vote. As the Civil Rights Act became
law in June 1964, the issue of discrimination and
the right to vote became another major focus for
the civil rights activist.

Dr. King tried to explain to his followers that
with political action they could change their destiny.

They could make sure that individuals like "Bull" Connor did not become public safety commissioner, and they could vote into office those people who would uphold their rights. They could make sure that enough money was allocated for blacks for schools, and they could demand—and get— such municipal services as having their garbage picked up.

SNCC had been working in the South since the early 1960s, integrating lunch counters and marching for desegregation. Many of SNCC's members were students, often aggressive and determined, and willing to risk their lives for the cause.

With the passage of the Civil Rights Act of 1964, SNCC took on the task of helping blacks in Selma to register. Naturally afraid of white retribution, Selma blacks needed to know that if they took on this battle, they would be protected. SNCC workers convinced them that this struggle was perhaps the most important one. They had a right to register to vote.*

Dr. King, on his way back from receiving the Nobel Peace Prize that brought him international recognition, decided, "We will probably have demonstrations in the near future in Alabama and

*The battle to register to vote was so heated that in 1964 it was a major factor in the murder of three young men who took part in what was called Freedom Summer. Andrew Goodman and Michael Schwerner (two whites) and James Chaney (a black) had been working for SNCC in the voter registration drive. One day they disappeared. The killers—among them a Philadelphia, Mississippi, deputy sheriff—had beaten and shot the men, then hidden their bodies. A fictionalized version of this incident is the subject of a film, *Mississippi Burning*, released in 1988.

Mississippi based around the right to vote." He added that he hoped that, where needed, federal marshals would be sent into the South to escort blacks to register.

In 1965, speaking to a crowd of about one thousand, he said,

> *We will seek to arouse the federal government by marching by the thousands to the places of registration. . . . When we get the right to vote, we will send to the statehouse not men who will stand in the doorways of universities to keep Negroes out, but men who will uphold the cause of justice.*[1]

Dr. King went to Selma, where plans were underway for marches and demonstrations to show the nation what black men and women had to endure to exercise their constitutional right to register to vote.

When King led the marchers to the Selma courthouse, he was arrested. The news only furthered the cause of the demonstrations. Five hundred students marched to the courthouse when they heard of his arrest. All five hundred were jailed. The news spread quickly, and, as in so many times in the past, the police acted brutally. As the national press covered these incidents, the news reached some of the right people. Outraged by the violence, a Congressional delegation traveled to Selma to investigate the voting rights practices.

It was a contradiction. With the passage of the Civil Rights Act of 1964, some thought that a major battle had been won, but others noted that more blacks were in jail in Selma then on the voter registration rolls.

The violence continued, and each demonstration got predictably more violent. White extremists stopped at nothing. Even an NBC news reporter, along with dozens of others, was badly beaten. One man, Jimmie Lee Jackson, was shot and later died.

The day of Jackson's funeral, Dr. King declared his support for a 50-mile march from Selma, across the Edmund Pettus Bridge spanning the Alabama River, and down Route 80 to Montgomery, the state capital. The march would take at least four days.

As one civil rights worker remembered, "We had decided that we were going to get killed or we was going to be free."[2] Others also recalled that their feeling was that things had gone on too long and had gone too far. Too many people had suffered and died. Now those committed to the struggle expressed their willingness to go as far as they had to to achieve equality.

John Lewis, a former SNCC leader, now serving as a member of Congress from Georgia, put it this way: "Too many funerals . . . people with courage and dignity gave the supreme sacrifice, really paid the supreme price."[3]

As the march began, led by SNCC's John Lewis, no police were in sight. However, when the marchers reached the bridge, they saw the Alabama State Troopers armed with billy clubs and tear gas. The troopers advanced, knocking the first dozen demonstrators off their feet. Tear gas was fired into the crowd, as troopers on horseback charged into the ranks of marchers. As one demonstrator remembers, "The horses . . . were more humane than the troopers, they stepped over fallen victims."[4]

Andrew Young, who is now the mayor of Atlanta, remembered, "The police were riding along on horseback beating people. . . . The tear gas was so thick that you couldn't get to where the people were who needed help. . . ."[5]

That night regularly scheduled television programs were interrupted by news bulletins showing the marchers being beaten and tear-gassed. It looked like war.

The march was stalemated. Alabama's governor George Wallace was unbending in his opposition to the march, and King was holding back from any attempt to continue it.

Many of King's followers were surprised. Orloff Miller, a minister from Boston, was quoted as saying, "Are we not going through with this confrontation? What's happening?" Some felt that King had betrayed them, but later King explained that he was going to go on with the march only if there was no police violence. King begged those who had come to Selma for the march to stay on while he went to Montgomery for a court hearing.

In Montgomery U.S. District Judge Frank M. Johnson, Jr., ruled that the protestors had the legal right to march from Selma to Montgomery.

President Johnson, giving unconditional support, sent the Alabama National Guard to watch over the march and also dispatched two thousand Army troops, one hundred FBI agents, and another hundred federal marshals.

The march got under way again. Angry segregationists, holding up signs saying "Yankee Trash Go Home," lined the route as King and Rabbi

Abraham Heschel of the Jewish Theological Seminary led the marchers. That day, four thousand people, black and white, made the 50-mile journey from Selma to Montgomery.

· · · · ·

On March 15, 1965, President Johnson announced his proposal for a voting rights act. "What happened in Selma was an American tragedy." He announced that he would send to Congress a bill that would "strike down all restrictions used to deny the people the right to vote." He added, "Their cause must be our cause, too. Because it's not Negroes, but it's really all of us who must overcome the crippling legacy of bigotry and injustice."

Violence continued even after the president's speech. But a major victory was won. Blacks at last had gained the right to be a part of democracy. Rosa Parks, the woman who started the Montgomery bus boycott, and Dr. King were present as President Johnson signed the bill into law.

The decade spanning the *Brown* decision of 1954 and the Voting Rights Act of 1965 saw more social change, more court decisions, and more legislation in the name of civil rights than any decade in our nation's history, according to author Juan Williams.

Following the passage of the Voting Rights Act, major gains took place for blacks, and some blacks became public officials. One particularly significant appointment was President Johnson's naming Thurgood Marshall, one of the pioneers in the civil rights movement, to be the first black on the Supreme Court.

*Dr. Martin Luther King, Jr., (center) leads
an estimated crowd of ten thousand or more
civil rights marchers on the last leg of their
Selma-to-Montgomery march in 1965.*

· · · · ·

The late sixties saw a different kind of civil rights movement as the struggle moved from the South to the North.

The mood of the country had shifted. The demand for equality was no longer demonstrated in marches. Dr. King had been considered by many to represent the more moderate wing of the civil rights movement: he advocated nonviolence and had taken his struggle through the proper legislative channels. Now he was losing the support of black youths, who wanted far more than the right to sit in the front of the bus. They wanted full citizenship—equal jobs, equal housing, equal opportunity in every walk of life.

They wanted power—black power. Malcolm X, the outspoken Black Muslim leader and a more radical Northern counterpart to Dr. King, was assassinated. Names like Stokely Carmichael, H. Rap Brown, Eldridge Cleaver, and Huey P. Newton became household words. "Burn, Baby, Burn" became the battle cry for many who no longer had faith in society as they knew it.

They questioned whether, in a fundamentally racist society, blacks would ever be treated as equals. Like dozens of Northern city ghettos, Watts, a black section of Los Angeles, was set on fire as frustrated youths took to the streets in defiance of

Black power advocates Stokely Carmichael (left) and H. Rap Brown (right) talk to newsmen during a 1968 protest against Columbia University's "racist policies."

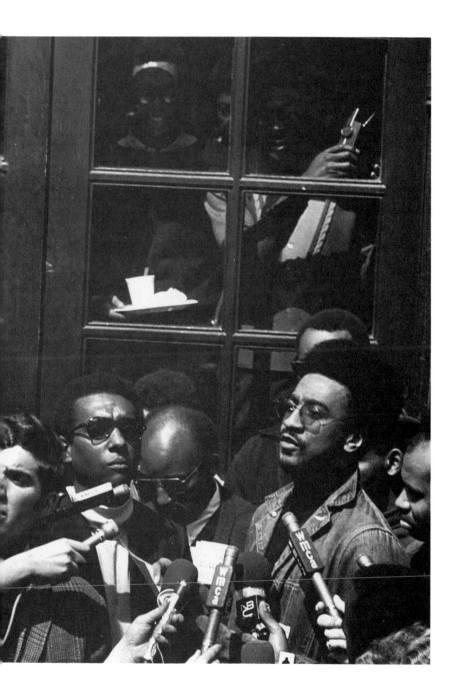

ghetto life. The cities burned because, to some, living in the ghetto was no longer acceptable as a way of life for poor blacks. Where and how they lived was clearly inferior to whites. Most lived in terrible conditions, in roach- and rat-infested, run-down houses.

Many Americans feared these new militant groups. They represented something unknown, and their goals were less comprehensible to those who supported the civil rights movement as long as it was tied to such issues as the right of blacks to use public facilities or the right to vote. Some of these militant groups, while relatively small in size, had enormous influence on the changes that continued to occur, if for no other reason than that many whites feared them. Dealing with Dr. King seemed like an easier task than dealing with militant blacks who called whites "devils" or "racist pigs."

On April 4, 1968, in Memphis, Tennessee, Dr. King was murdered. It shocked the nation into mourning. This further angered blacks and whites frustrated by the country's racism. There seemed to be little hope for a peaceful resolution to the race problem.

That year the president appointed a commission to study race relations. The Kerner Commission found a country deeply divided by color—black and white. The commission also found that blacks were living far below the standard of whites, without the same opportunities in education, in employment, and in housing.

By the time the Johnson era had come to an end, new legislation had been signed into law and a war on poverty had been declared, creating anti-poverty programs and affirmative action plans that offered new opportunities for blacks, including some of the most far-reaching educational opportunities thus far. With access to a better education, more blacks were now able to get better jobs, to join the middle class, to realize the American dream.

· · · · ·

As blacks began to achieve some semblance of equality, other groups who had suffered discrimination and injustice began to raise their voices, too. American women, American Indians, Hispanics, the disabled, the elderly, gays, and other minority groups, taking their lessons from the civil rights movement, also began to call for equal pay, equal employment, equal education opportunities, equal treatment. Perhaps they didn't realize it at the time, but those who were a part of the civil rights movement were blazing a trail that others would follow.

5

FOLLOWING IN THE PATH OF THE MOVEMENT

In the 1960s the sociologist Gunnar Myrdal wrote, "As the Negro was awarded his place in society, so there was a woman's place. . . . The myth of the 'Contented Woman' who did not want to have suffrage or other civil rights and equal opportunities had the same social function as the myth of the 'Contented Negro.' "[1]

In 1966 Betty Friedan and a dozen or so other activists founded the National Organization for Women (NOW), a sort of NAACP for women. NOW's founders had concluded that the Civil Rights Act of 1964, which banned job discrimination on the basis of gender as well as race, religion, and national origin, would not be enough to prod government agencies to act on complaints of violations. NOW's motto was clear and simple: "Full equality for all women in America in truly equal partnership with men, now."

Undoubtedly, the civil rights movement inspired the women's movement because women also saw themselves as a class of people shut out of the American system, just as blacks had been. NOW's intention never was to subvert male powers, but to work through the legislatures, the courts, and through grass root organizations to achieve equality in education, in employment, and in politics. Women wanted equal treatment and equal opportunities in all aspects of life.

In 1968 only 28 million women worked outside the home. Of these less than 7 percent were doctors, only 3 percent lawyers, and less than 1 percent were engineers. Over 90 percent earned less than five thousand dollars per year, while the remaining 10 percent earned 40 percent less than men.

As former congresswoman Barbara Jordan pointed out, the civil rights movement challenged the way blacks were treated in this country, so, logically, other groups raised the same questions about *their* civil rights.

While the "women's movement" concentrated on the issues of wages and opportunities in the workplace, it also raised the issue of reproductive freedom: the right to bear children and the legal right to have an abortion (otherwise known as "pro choice"). Eleanor Smeal, former president of NOW, put it as follows: "There is no liberty for women if they can't control their own fertility."[2] In 1973, in the case of *Roe* v. *Wade,* women won that freedom in the Supreme Court. In that decision the Court ruled that women had the legal right to have an abortion and that they had the right to choose to have a child. In other words they did have the right of control over their own bodies.

Next, women challenged pay equity. They set out to change the image of women as being lesser than men, in terms of employment, education, and even in terms of language. In fact, sexism in language became a major issue of the women's movement, as women fought against gender-specific terms like postman, fireman, and chairman. The appellation *Ms.* gradually came into general use as women resisted being categorized by their relationship to a man (*Mrs.*—a man's wife; *Miss*—no man's wife). Women wanted to establish credit for themselves, too, under their own name, something that was almost impossible twenty years ago.

As with the civil rights movement for blacks, some of the goals of the 1960s women's movement have now been achieved and incorporated into the fabric of our society. Thanks to the women's movement most American women take for granted that they can control their own fertility. It is now also a part of our culture to see women in higher education, in Olympic sports, and in fields that used to be the exclusive domain of men, such as law, medicine, and engineering. In the holding of political office as well, women, along with blacks, have made great strides. In 1986 nineteen women ran for governor, and over eleven hundred were state legislators. As improbable as it was for John Lewis, the former leader of SNCC, to imagine that one day he would be a member of Congress and that the Reverend Jesse Jackson would be a presidential candidate, it was a major historic event for Geraldine Ferraro to be the vice-presidential candidate in 1984 on the Democratic ticket.

· · · · ·

Because so much has changed in this country for blacks and for women, so much is now taken for granted. Those born after the 1960s cannot truly appreciate how our entire way of life is different today. If blacks take for granted that they can vote without fear of reprisals or that they can run for president, women now take for granted that they are part of the work force, that they can run for high office, that they are no longer viewed as mothers and wives only, dependent on their husbands for their survival.

Today the issues are different ones. Women can go to law school, become attorneys, and practice law. We see them daily, dressed in suits, going to work, and taking on major responsibilities in the marketplace. They can get credit on their own and build their own financial security. But that's only part of the picture.

The fact is that millions of American women are not doing so well. There is still a major discrepancy in wages. According to the U.S. Census Bureau, women still earn only sixty-one cents for every dollar paid to men. Most gainfully employed women still cluster in the low-paying, sex-segregated jobs like nursing, teaching, or secretarial positions, sometimes called the "pink collar ghetto" jobs. Women and children are the poorest segment of our society, and their number is growing. Three out of five adults officially designated as below the poverty line are women. Half of the poor families in America are headed by a woman. Minority women and their children are the most disadvantaged group in America. Two-thirds of the children in black and Hispanic communities come from households headed by a single woman.

The Reagan Years, as some have come to call the years 1981–1989, were not good for minorities or women. Many of the social programs that gave a boost to civil rights and helped blacks and other minorities were slowly eliminated, particularly the programs that helped the families of poor and working women. Such programs included food stamps, day care, and AFDC (Aid to Families with Dependent Children).

The challenge for the women's movement today, as in the civil rights movement, is to find ways for those most in need to become part of the system. While twenty years ago the women's movement advocated freedom for women to be what they wanted to be, to be single or married, free to explore new options, today we find that most women are still responsible for child care and only a small percentage of the responsibility is shared by men. Therefore, while the women's movement struggled to get pay equity for women, most women still find that they are restricted from assuming the same positions as men; the reason is that women cannot travel as freely or take advantage of the training opportunities that some companies offer because they cannot afford day care for their children.

In 1978 NOW and other organizations achieved a major victory for women, the Pregnancy Discrimination Act, which prohibits employers from firing a woman solely because she is pregnant. Today NOW and other civil rights groups are fighting to establish the right of all people to take a four-month leave from their job, be they pregnant or not. As NOW president Eleanor Smeal explained,

Our worry is protective labor legislation. In the past, it was used not to hire women. . . . Our fear is that what appears to be a benefit will be

used against us. If a person is disabled—male or female—she should be able to take a four-month leave without pay and not be fired.[3]

America is way behind in the issue of day care. Most European countries provide subsidized day care, job protection, and paid maternity leave. In those countries the gap between gender and wage has been narrowing, while in our country the wage gap is about the same as it was in 1939.

In 1938 Supreme Court Justice Felix Frankfurter made some profound observations about the struggle for equal rights for women:

> *The legal position of women cannot be stated in a single, simple formula, because her life cannot be expressed in a single, simple relation. Women's legal status necessarily involves complicated formulations, because a woman occupies many relations. The law must have regard for woman in her manifold relations as an individual, as a wage earner, as a wife, as a mother, as a citizen.*[4]

The 1960s were a pivotal time for challenging our system and the rights of individuals within that system. If the women's movement was inspired in part by the civil rights movement and the Civil Rights Act of 1964, the same can be said for the gay rights movement as well as for support for the disabled, for Native Americans, for all of those who feel that they have been discriminated against because of their race, sex, color, handicap, or religion. In education, employment, and housing, the Civil Rights Act had a profound impact on all these groups. In all these areas discrimination is against the law. Today, as part of the normal course of business, corporations must submit a written statement to the government that they adhere to the law. While no doubt many will argue that there is still discrimination in employment and in housing, the fact remains that discrimination of any kind is against the law.

If the goals and objectives of these groups were separate in the past, today there is greater recognition that the rights of one group have a direct relationship to those of another. If one group can be discriminated against, then all of us can become victims of discrimination. Gay rights organizations and women's groups have a greater understanding that if they join together to fight against discrimination, they have a better chance of achieving equal treatment for everyone. The Reverend Jesse Jackson has addressed many of the existing inadequacies, and many of these concerns were voiced in the 1988 Democratic party platform. In the past twenty years, over a thousand cases concerning discrimination of one form or another have been taken to court.

Few would argue that the victories won by the equal rights advocates have formed the foundation for the mainstream ideology of the Democratic

The civil rights movement inspired other advocate groups striving for equality. Here, parents of gays show support for their sons and daughters at the Gay Pride Festival Parade in West Hollywood, California, in 1986.

MY DAUGHTER
IS LESBIAN
AND THAT'S OK
IF YOU'RE
IF YOU'RE
THAT'S OK,
HEART
OUR
GAY CHILDREN

party. The victories that took place over the past twenty years are no longer considered newsworthy. To those who were born after 1964, it is normal to see their mothers go to work, to see a woman judge or doctor, or to see a black person hosting the democratic convention—as was the case in 1988. A common sight on TV is women newscasters, blacks in the roles of doctors and lawyers in dramas and situation comedies, and the disabled, all represented as part of society. This is what the younger TV viewer has always known. But in reality these changes are very recent. This is a different country from the one we knew twenty years ago.

6

WE STILL
HAVE A LONG
WAY TO GO

"People often separate politics from everyday life,
not understanding that politics is everyday life,"
according to Menges, a film director who has
concentrated on political subjects. Or, as a former
civil rights worker reflected, "A movement for
social change should be judged by the degree and
amount of social change it accomplishes." So, if we
are to judge the civil rights movement and what it
has accomplished, we must also examine what type
of social changes and attitudes we have today.

Roger Wilkins, a journalist and expert on the
civil rights era, commented, "We have done the easy
part. We have made opportunities for the blacks for
whom it was easy to provide opportunity."[1] Robert
L. Woodson put it this way, "Those blacks who were
prepared to walk through the doors of opportunity
benefited. But many who sacrificed the most, the
poor blacks, benefited least from the changes."[2]

The 1980s have brought back some of the
memories of the 1960s. In the past year racial

violence has doubled. In 1988, in New York City alone, over two hundred incidents of violent racial incidents were reported.

In 1987, New York, not Selma or Birmingham, was the scene of the kind of violence that we used to see or hear about twenty years earlier. Five white teenagers participated in what was termed a "race riot." They confronted three black men in the borough of Queens, outside a pizza shop in the white neighborhood of Howard Beach, savagely attacked them, and chased one of them, Michael Griffith, into the path of an oncoming car. He was struck and killed. It shocked the neighborhood; it shocked the nation. The "savage attack" that started by name-calling and racial slurs ended in tragedy. The death of Michael Griffith struck a chord in the minds of those who remembered the South twenty years ago.

The incident seemed especially frightening because those white teenagers would seem to be far removed in time from those who witnessed blacks beaten and even lynched because of their race. What was different from twenty years ago—when Emmett Till was killed by white men—was the outcome. This time the jury found several of the defendants guilty of manslaughter and sentenced them to prison. The case is being appealed, however, because some of the defendants claim that the black men provoked racial tension.

About the same time the *New York Times* reported that neo-Nazi activities were on the rise among young people. So-called skinheads, numbering more than two thousand, are believed to be deliberately fomenting racial incidents. These white supremacists openly express their dislike of blacks and other minorities.

In a separate incident Tawana Brawley, a fifteen-year-old black living in upstate New York, was found in a fetal position inside a plastic bag, with *nigger* and *KKK* written in charcoal on her torso. New York State Attorney General Robert Abrams conducted an extensive investigation and concluded that the entire incident had been fabricated, but the idea of these epithets being marked on her body was shocking. Some people still believe that Ms. Brawley was brutally attacked and that a cover-up took place.

In another case, also in upstate New York, the body of a black teenager was found with *KKK* carved on her body. It seemed too similar to incidents that had taken place twenty years ago.

Charles B. Rangel, a senior congressman from New York, wrote in the *New York Times*,

> *Howard Beach was really about racism. There is no way of getting around that. But neither Howard Beach nor New York City has a corner on that market. Nevertheless, in the post mortem of this case, we would be remiss not to give serious thought to the deep divisions between the black and white communities as well as to the social and economic issues this case raises. [He went on to say,] New York City is in the midst of a social crisis. This . . . is the sense of hopelessness and helplessness of those perched on the lower end of the ladder. Many of these people happen to be blacks and Hispanics. Convinced that they have been bypassed and forgotten they feel as if they have nothing to lose.*[3]

Twenty years after the 1964 Civil Rights Act, sociologist William Julius Wilson wrote, "A troubling dilemma confronts proponents of racial equality and social justice."[4] A black underclass has emerged and conditions in the inner-city ghettos have deteriorated despite civil rights victories. What went wrong? According to Wilson, structural changes in this country related to the economy created some of the conditions in the inner city. Specifically, the types of manufacturing jobs commonly held by minorities have shrunk while the types of jobs requiring greater training and skills have increased. Therefore, those in the ghettos are finding themselves unemployed—and unemployable. According to this view, joblessness is the main reason that more and more urban blacks are finding themselves outside the social order and are enduring poverty, poor health, and, sometimes, homelessness.

Wilson discovered that in the five largest cities—New York, Detroit, Chicago, Los Angeles, and Philadelphia—the number of people living in poverty increased by 22 percent between 1970 and 1980, although the cities' total population had decreased by 9 percent. Not surprisingly he found that the poor were clustered in specific areas, isolating them from other, more prosperous neighborhoods. Therefore, "Social isolation implies that contact between groups of different class or racial background is either lacking or has become increasingly intermittent."[5] Estimates of the actual number of people in the *underclass* vary, but at least seven or eight million people are believed to be a part of this population. Wilson believes that a real revolution has occurred for many blacks, but the poor have in effect dropped off the political screens."

It makes sense. The black middle class significantly increased as they moved to different neighborhoods and found better housing or moved to newly integrated areas, leaving those living in the ghettos in isolation.

The people in the ghettos were also left with fewer role models. Many found themselves unable to secure jobs other than very low-paying, menial ones which did not enable them to support a family or to pay for decent housing. Today, as a result, nearly one in three black children has no working parent.

Simultaneously, according to the U.S. Department of Education, black student enrollment in four-year colleges peaked at 10.2 percent in 1976. By 1982 that figure had dropped to 9.6 percent. College enrollment for blacks continued to decline steadily, as government programs dwindled and college tuition rose to staggering proportions. Reversing the policies of the 1960s, colleges have recruited fewer and fewer students from the inner cities. Black professors now constitute only 1 percent of all faculty in predominantly white colleges.[6]

Urban school desegregation has made little progress, according to researchers at the University of Chicago. "There are millions of fewer white children and many more children from minority communities in public schools than in the past. . . . Only 3 percent of white students now attend school in central school districts."

In New York City, for example, the school attended by a typical black student is 60 percent black, 27 percent Hispanic, 6 percent white, and 3 percent Asian. In some of the inner-city school districts, black and Hispanic students have the highest school dropout rate, consequently creating a crisis of unemployment or underemployment. Furthermore, in 1988, a New York State task force

found that New York has two distinct school systems, one that is white and affluent and another that is poor and largely black and Hispanic. The Task Force on Education of Children and Youth at Risk concluded that racism clearly underlies much of the problem.

If the 1980s frequently remind us of the 1960s, Yonkers may be one of the reasons. In 1985 this middle-class, predominantly white city in New York State, less than an hour from New York City, was ordered by the courts to build low-income housing units in mostly white neighborhoods by March of 1989, and to build eight hundred units at a later date for families earning between $13,000 and $32,000 a year. In 1988, after repeated appeals by city officials to overturn the decision, the U.S. Supreme Court ruled not to hear their appeal, declaring that the city intentionally and unlawfully promoted racial segregation in housing and education. The ruling meant that Yonkers had lost its last chance of avoiding the disputed desegregation plan. A New York judge started fining the city of Yonkers and its City Council on a daily basis, threatening the city with bankruptcy.

While some Yonkers officials claimed that their defiance was not racially motivated, but rather was

Top: Luxurious houses and lawns characterize the residential area of southwest Atlanta, home to upwardly mobile blacks; while in Harlem (bottom), a ghetto family huddles around the stove for warmth. The contrast reveals the widening rift between the impoverished poor and the emerging middle class in black society.

based on their concern that building low-income housing would reduce property values and radically change their middle-class neighborhoods, their defiance of the government was a reminder of Governor Wallace and other Southern politicians defying the law in the 1960s.

Only after the fines were levied against the city and bankruptcy loomed did the City Council agree to go forward with plans for low-income housing.

• • • • •

Today we again see black college students demonstrating against school policies. These demonstrations are different from those of the sixties. Then blacks were fighting for the right to enroll. Now, however, students at such prestigious colleges as Dartmouth and Stanford are demonstrating against rising tuition costs and apartheid in South Africa, urging their schools to divest themselves of financial interest in American companies doing business there. They are also demonstrating against the Western orientation of their education, which often excludes black or Third World philosophers and their ideologies.

At the University of Massachusetts, a twenty-year-old student pointed out in an interview with *The New York Times*, "racism is prevalent here. People could afford an education if they took a year off." Now, he says, tuition costs hurt minorities, and he was picketing against the rising costs.

A black man stands next to a flier denouncing housing desegregation in Yonkers, New York.

Certainly, the inability of black youth to share proportionately in college enrollment and employment opportunities is a problem not only for them and their families, but for the larger economy as well. If we are to compete internationally, we'll need people in the work force with the skills required to meet the challenge. According to New York City Mayor Koch's Commission on Black New Yorkers, an estimated 124,000 young New Yorkers are dropouts at a time when there are only 26,000 job openings for people with less than a high school education.

In 1987 only 34 percent of blacks in the labor force had one or more years of college compared with 46 percent of white workers. While blacks were 13.8 percent of the high school graduates, they were only 9.4 percent of college freshmen. Today, only one-quarter of black high school graduates eighteen to twenty-four years of age are in college, compared with over a third of white high school graduates.

At the same time it is predicted that over the next decade job opportunities will be greater in high-paying white-collar jobs, those that require a good education. While overall employment projections are for an increase of 19 percent, executive and administrative positions and other management catagories will expand by 29 percent. Currently, those holding these positions have at least one to six years of college education. Therefore, the prospects for those who do not attend college are limited.

Clearly, if the federal programs that in the past have helped encourage the disadvantaged to obtain higher education are discontinued, black youth face an uncertain future.

The greatest disparity in employment between blacks and whites in 1987 was among people under the age of twenty-five. Black youths seeking jobs were twice as likely as white youths not to be hired. Only one-quarter of all black youths ages sixteen to nineteen held a job in 1987. Only 57 percent of blacks, compared with 70 percent of whites, were in the labor force during that year. Undoubtedly, the gap between blacks and whites over the next decade will widen if a larger proportion of the jobs require higher education and training.

In Chicago, according to one study, one in ten whites was considered "poor"; in the black community, one in three; and in the Hispanic community, one in four.

While the 1980s have shown signs of some very troubling problems emerging for the black and Hispanic communities, with heightened racial tension and demonstrations and violence on the rise, these incidences are relatively few and far between. And while poverty has increased, so has the awareness that serious attention must be given to remedy the situation.

As the Reverend Joseph E. Lowery, the civil rights leader and former associate of Dr. King, put it, "We won the battle to sit on the customer's side of the lunch counter, but we are still fighting the battle to get on the cash register side of the counter."

Twenty-six years ago a quarter of a million people attended the March on Washington and heard Dr. King deliver his "I Have a Dream" speech on the steps of the Lincoln Memorial. In 1988, his widow, Coretta Scott King, organized a similar march on Washington. She said, "We have much to do before Dr. King's dream will be fulfilled. Eight million Americans have been added to the poverty rolls since 1963. Discrimination persists in many areas. We have no choice but to march on Washington again."

The day before the 1988 march, an editorial in *The New York Times* read,

> *It is significant that one of Dr. King's greatest victories was that his nonviolent integrationist vision of civil rights has survived as the mainstream movement. . . . Toward the end of his life, Dr. King said, "We are not interested in being integrated into this value structure. . . . Our economy must become more person centered than property oriented.*

Twenty-six years ago Dr. Martin Luther King argued that American society needed basic changes in structure, to include the masses of people who are poor and without hope. "True compassion is more than just flinging a coin to a beggar. It is recognizing that a system that produces beggars, needs restructuring."

7

WHAT HAS CHANGED?

Former Congresswoman Barbara Jordan, reflecting on the civil rights movement, said,

> *The civil rights movement called America to look at itself in a giant mirror. It said to America, look at what you have been saying to us all these years. Do the black people who were born on this soil, who are American citizens, do they really feel this is the land of opportunity, land of the free. . . . America had to say no.*

On February 29, 1968, President Johnson appointed Governor Otto Kerner of Illinois to head a commission on the causes of racial riots that had swept the country. The commission came back with a disturbing finding. It warned that the United States was "moving towards two societies, one black, one white—separate and unequal." The commission blamed white racism for polarization. They argued that only a "compassionate, massive and sustained government effort could reverse the overall trend."

The Kerner report had a profound impact on the next two decades. The government did make major efforts to correct the wrongs of society. Numerous training programs were started, and higher education for blacks increased from 6 to 11 percent from 1968 to 1976.

Now, looking back on the last twenty years, we can see that an intriguing picture has emerged. Things have radically changed. This society, in a very short time, has undergone a real revolution. However, the report card is far from perfect. Though remarkable progress has been made, integration is far from a reality. Race is still an issue.

The percentage of blacks earning more than $35,000 a year rose from 15.7 percent in 1970 to 21.2 percent in 1986, according to government statistics. The average income for blacks has increased, with 8.8 percent of blacks earning more than $50,000 a year. Clearly, a solid black middle class has emerged. But the gap between the income of black and white families has been widening since the mid-1970s. Black median income is 57 percent that of whites, a decline of about 4 percentage points since the early 1970s. Today, three times as many blacks live in poverty. In 1986 one in three blacks, as compared with one in ten whites, still lived below the poverty line—$11,203 for a family of four.[1]

When it comes to where we live, integration is clearly far from a reality. We still live in separate and different communities. In 1980, 31 percent of blacks lived in neighborhoods that were 90 percent or more black, while six out of ten whites lived in neighborhoods that were essentially white. In fact, housing is still the single most segregated aspect of American life today.

If a solid black middle class has indisputably emerged (better educated, better paid, and generally living better), so has another group—the socially disabled poor, which some refer to as the "underclass." There is an estimated population of 2.5 million of them today, three times that of what it was in the 1970s. The members of this group are usually unemployed, often rely on welfare, and frequently drop out of school. A significant number of families is headed by a female parent. The rate of unemployment for black youths is more than double that of white youths, while crimes of violence are disproportionately higher, as is teenage pregnancy, with an infant mortality rate for blacks twice that for whites.

But as gloomy as the picture of this growing underclass is, the number of elected black officials is equally significant. If we think back on the past twenty years, we remember Governor George Wallace blocking the entrance to the University of Alabama and police beating black marchers. Today, in contrast, we can point to seven thousand black elected officials, including over three hundred mayors of major cities, like Los Angeles and Atlanta, compared with less than a hundred black elected officials in 1955. Still, while blacks make up 11 percent of the population, only 1.3 percent of our elected officials are black.

The Reverend Jesse Jackson ran in second place for the Democratic nomination for president, something that was unthinkable twenty years ago. William H. Gray III, a Pennsylvania congressman,

The Reverend Jesse Jackson gives
his supporters the thumbs-up sign before
formally announcing his candidacy
for president of the United States.

is the chairman of the Budget Committee, a powerful position with a major impact on this country's allocation of resources. Andrew Young, now Atlanta's mayor, served as chief ambassador to the United Nations, a first in history.

Young's city, Atlanta, most clearly signifies some of the gains for blacks. Today, 45 percent of blacks are middle class, as opposed to 13 percent twenty years ago, yet blacks and whites live in different parts of town. Blacks live on the south side, whites mostly on the north side, a pattern that developed over ten years ago when many whites fled the city as blacks moved in. The poor blacks live in neither area—because they can't afford to.

As Congressman Gray observed, the civil rights issues are different from those of twenty years ago.

> The issue is no longer, can you check into the hotel? It's whether you've got the money to check out. The issue is no longer whether you can go to the University of Mississippi, but whether you can pay the tuition. The issue is no longer where you sit on the bus or whether you can drive it; it's whether you can develop the capital to own the bus company.[2]

The old battles to register blacks to vote are behind us. Certainly, registered black voters have made their presence felt. Over 2 million black people were registered to vote between 1980 and 1984, an increase of 24 percent. Today, all politicians recognize that they cannot win an election in a city with a significant black population without the black vote. Furthermore, in 1987, 80 percent of blacks who voted, voted for the Democratic party, giving many Democratic candidates a strong edge in inner-city areas.

Progress has continued for some blacks, while not for others. While income for blacks has increased among the top 20 percent of wage earners, it has decreased for the bottom 20 percent. Between the years 1960 and 1970, the black middle class grew a startling 107 percent. Among the upper group, from 1970 to 1986, the percentage doubled to 9 percent for those earning $50,000 or more. In the mid-1980s, 47 percent owned homes compared with 67 percent of whites, yet a black home was worth $20,000 less than a nonblack house. Today 13 percent of whites are employed as executives or managers. This figure is half for blacks.

So the answer to the question, "What has changed in the last twenty years since the Kerner report?" is not so simple or straightforward. A lot has changed.

As Eleanor Holmes Norton, former head of the Equal Employment Opportunities Commission, observed, referring to the spectacular showing by Jesse Jackson in the presidential primaries:

> *Twenty years ago, I would not have predicted that any black man could have made a credible run for the presidency. [She added,] I would not have predicted such a large number of black mayors of the big cities, that a black man would become the head of the Budget Committee, or that there would be a black ambassador to the United Nations. We are literally in the first*

*generation of black success after twenty genera-
tions in this country.*[3]

Clearly, the greatest success of Martin Luther King
and the civil rights movement was the achievement
of legal equality and legislation that outlawed discrimination. Such an achievement cannot be under-
estimated. The programs that evolved after the
Kerner report were successful to some degree in
giving parity to blacks through education and training programs.

However, full economic parity has not been
achieved. And the past eight years of Ronald
Reagan's administration have reversed much of the
progress of the 1970s. The poet June Jordan had
some harsh words for what happened in the late
1980s:

> *In the '60s we didn't have Ronald Reagan, I
> think that cannot be underestimated. I mean
> Him, quite personally, and I also mean the
> people he represents. He has legitimatized a
> depthness of egoism and cruelty of perspective
> and meanness of spirit that is unprecedented in
> our lifetime. I think that people feel encouraged
> now to be racist.*[4]

Vernon Jordan, former president of the National
Urban League (one of the most prestigious civil
rights organizations), also sounded a note of pessi-
mism. He said that this last administration promoted the notion of self help, that is, pulling
oneself up by one's bootstraps, something that
blacks obviously have difficulty in accomplishing

since so often they have nothing to hold on to. According to Jordan, the leadership of Ronald Reagan has shifted the mood of the country away from support of civil rights for blacks and other minorities and for women.

If we look at the civil rights movement and its accomplishments, we would have to give it high marks on many fronts. Yes, blacks now account for a large number of people who vote; therefore, they have a partnership in this country. They can vote people into and out of office. In fact, for the 1984 election, Jesse Jackson was responsible in large part for getting out the black vote. And since 80 percent of blacks are Democrats, the large turnout of blacks made it possible for Democrats to regain control of the Senate.

In the 1988 election Democratic presidential candidate Michael Dukakis knew that he needed the black vote and attended the March on Washington. Although Dukakis lost the election, the Democrats continued to hold the majority in Congress with the help of the black vote.

If we look at school desegregation, the results were, at best, mixed. Those who lived in integrated areas usually went to integrated schools. But most housing remained segregated, even though a *Newsweek* poll indicated that both blacks and whites would prefer to live in a neighborhood that is mixed, half and half, and only 33 percent of whites claimed to wish to live with whites only.

While in the last twenty years marriages between blacks and whites have doubled, they still constitute only 1.5 percent of marriages, possibly an indication that on a personal level this society is not ready to be color-blind.

8

THE NEXT
FRONTIER

Jesse Jackson did not win the Democratic nomination but he came far closer than any black ever. In the process, he made himself a hero to many, but that is only half the story. His success depends on much more than his extraordinary skills. It reflects two dramatic decades in which blacks have deepened and broadened their political consciousness and involvement. His success is a triumph also for history.

The New York Times
August 1988

The 1988 Democratic convention was in a sense the culmination of an era. Twenty-five years before, in 1963, in Selma, Alabama, civil rights workers were beaten to the ground for peacefully marching against voting rights discrimination and for the right to vote. The next year Fannie Lou Hamer and the "Freedom Democratic party" challenged the whites-only Mississippi delegation of the Democratic party and demanded to be seated at the convention. A bitter fight between the Freedom Democratic party and the all-white Mississippi delegation erupted at the 1964 Democratic convention, when Fannie Lou Hamer declared, "If the Freedom Democratic party is not seated now, I question America. Is this America? The land of the free and the home of the brave?" If Mrs. Hamer had been alive in 1989, twenty-five years later, she would have seen her fight to get blacks seated as part of the Mississippi delegation realized. She would have seen significant changes. Now, 20 percent of the Democratic party is black. And the convention was held in Atlanta, a city with a black mayor and a 45 percent black middle-class population. The changes over the twenty-five years are most visible here.

In 1988 Jesse Jackson brought twelve hundred blacks, whites, Asians, and Hispanics to the convention as his delegates. In the presidential primaries, he won 92 percent of the black vote, an achievement far beyond the imagination of anyone who remembered the 1960s civil rights struggles.

Jackson, in delivering the keynote address, brought Rosa Parks to the podium, saying, "Welcome Rosa Parks, the woman who started the civil rights movement." Thousands of people on the convention floor rose to their feet and cheered the woman who refused to give up her seat on the bus some thirty-three years before.

For those who had witnessed the civil rights struggle of the past twenty-some years, the convention was mixed with irony. Nostalgia was part of this convention. Ann Richards, the treasurer of Texas, opened the convention, reminding the participants that only two women had ever addressed it: Barbara Jordan, the former congresswoman from Texas, and she.

Birmingham, Alabama, was vivid in many people's minds. They remembered Eugene "Bull" Connor, who ordered dogs and tear gas used against civil rights protestors. Today, the mayor of Birmingham is black, and so is the majority of the elected city officials. "Bull" Connor is history, a character in a story told to children.

As he spoke before the convention, Jackson passionately noted,

> *Martin Luther King, Jr., lies only a few miles from us tonight. Tonight he must feel good as he looks down upon us. We sit here together, a rainbow coalition—the sons and daughters of slaves sitting together around a common table, to decide the direction of our party and our country. His heart would be full.*

Mayor Andrew Young later said, "Jesse Jackson set the agenda for the 1988 [Democratic] campaign. . . . No matter who is elected, Jackson may be the big winner."

Jackson went on to tell the convention,

> *As a testament to the struggles of those who have gone before, as a legacy for those who will come after, as a tribute to the endurance, the patience, the courage of our forefathers and mothers, as an assurance that their prayers are being answered, their work has not been in vain and hope is eternal, tomorrow night my name will go into nomination for the presidency of the United States.*

Jackson did not win, but he came to the convention with twelve hundred delegates—a first in American history.

Jackson spoke not only to blacks. He talked about the struggles of women, still earning 60 percent of what men earn; about Hispanics, who used to be ashamed to talk in Spanish; about the gay community, urging people to have compassion for people with AIDS; about the disabled; the disadvantaged; the farmers. He said, "We form a great quilt of unity and common ground. We'll have the power to bring about health care and housing and jobs and education and hope. . . . We the people can win."

By law and daily practice, we are now an integrated society, yet large inequities still exist. The Democratic Convention of 1988 will go down in history as did the one in 1964. The 1964 convention was historic because blacks from Mississippi challenged the seating of white-only delegates from their state. The 1988 convention will be remembered for the role that Jesse Jackson and other blacks played in forming the party platform.

Many at the convention stated that twenty years before they never would have imagined that they would be watching a black man be nominated for the presidency. Today some 22 percent of blacks and about the same percentage of whites believe that in the next twenty years a black man could become president.[1] In 1988, while Jackson came in second in the Democratic primaries, he was also a consideration for the vice-presidency, a first in history. The Democratic convention was a reflection of how much we have really changed.

· · · · ·

The next frontier concerns the underclass, those who are not a part of the system, because they are disadvantaged, jobless, too poor to have a voice.

Progress is being made. For example, blacks make up 1.1 percent of employees at IBM, and 7 percent of its managers. Certainly this is enormous progress since the 1950s when IBM first began aggressively to recruit blacks. Or we can cite Richard D. Parsons, who is president of one of the largest banks in the country.

However, there is still a lot of ground to cover. Seventy percent of blacks and nearly 50 percent of whites do not believe that blacks get a fair shake. Most blacks believe that there should be more emphasis on integration. At the same time, on a personal level, over 50 percent of whites do not want their children married to blacks, and only 37 percent say they have entertained blacks in their homes. Most large-city schools are still not integrated. According to a recent poll by Media General-Associated Press, today 84 percent of those polled believe that the nation has moved closer to equality in the years since Dr. King spoke out, but 55 percent also stated that American society was racist overall.

The next frontier must address the problems of those still left out, those whose basic needs are still unfulfilled—decent housing, better education, and jobs.

How do we change the psychological perception that black life is not worth the same as white life? It is documented that blacks who kill whites receive the harshest punishment. How do we break the cycle of crime in the black community?

According to the U.S. Department of Justice

statistics, 18 percent of all black men will spend time behind prison bars; the statistic for white men is only 3 percent. According to all reports, blacks are far more likely to be arrested for serious crimes than whites. Blacks, who make up 12 percent of the population, commit 62 percent of robberies and 29 percent of burglaries. Blacks are also given longer sentences. Those in authority to pass judgment, such as state and federal judges, are still almost all white. Yet there has been some progress in the number of blacks who are police officers and correction officers—the figure has doubled since 1972.

While progress has been made for women in the workplace, with more career opportunities, higher wages, and more affordable day care, women and children—most of whom are black—are still the poorest members of our society. In order to "keep hope alive," as Jesse Jackson has urged us to do, we as a society have to attack this problem, so that the progress that has been made will have real meaning and significance to the millions who cannot do without welfare because they cannot afford day care for their children while they work, to those who have to live on the streets because they cannot afford a home.

We are not what we were, but we still have to do better to be what we must be—a society where all people have the same opportunities. Martin Luther King's dream was a far-reaching one, that

All God's children, black men and white men, Jews and gentiles, Protestants and Catholics, will be able to join hands and sing in the words of the old Negro spiritual, "Free at last. Free at last. Thank God Almighty, we are free at last."[2]

SOURCE NOTES

INTRODUCTION
1. "Poll Power," *Life: Special Issue. The Dream Then and Now*, vol. 11, no. 5 (Spring 1988), 34.
2. Oates, Stephen B., *Let the Trumpet Sound: The Life of Martin Luther King, Jr.* New York: NAL, 1983.
3. William Julius Wilson, *Truly Disadvantaged: The Inner City, the Underclass, & Public Policy* (Chicago: University of Chicago Press, 1987), 138.

CHAPTER ONE
1. Juan Williams, *Eyes on the Prize: America's Civil Rights Years, 1954–1965* (New York: Viking Press, 1987), 17.
2. Ibid., p. 20.; also see *Eyes on the Prize* documentary.
3. Ibid., 38.
4. *Eyes on the Prize*, documentary.

CHAPTER TWO
1. Printed on a flier distributed by the Montgomery Improvement Association.

CHAPTER THREE
1. Williams, op. cit., p. 132.
2. television news footage.
3. Williams, op. cit., 147.

4. television news footage: interviews with Freedom Riders.
5. *Eyes on the Prize*, 149; also see *Eyes on the Prize* documentary.
6. *Eyes on the Prize*, op. cit., 173.
7. Williams, op. cit., 195.
8. Ibid., 200.
9. Ibid., 226.

CHAPTER FOUR
1. Williams, op. cit., 258.
2. Ibid., 267.
3. Ibid., 226.
4. Ibid., 267.
5. Ibid., 269.

CHAPTER FIVE
1. Martha Lear, "The Second Feminist Wave," *New York Times Magazine*, March 10, 1968, 24.
2. Dorothy Wickenden, "What Now?," *The New Republic*, May 5, 1986, 20.
3. Ibid., 24.
4. Ibid., 25.

CHAPTER SIX
1. Personal interview.
2. *State of Black America*. television program, associate producer: Anna Kosof.
3. *New York Times*, December 29, 1987, 19.
4. Wilson, op. cit., 109
5. Ibid., 60.
6. "The Dwindling Black Presence on Campus," *New York Times Magazine*, April 27, 1986, 46.

CHAPTER SEVEN
1. Katherine McFate, ed., *Metropolitan Area Fact Book: A Statistical Portrait of Blacks and Whites*.
2. "The Next Step: Constituencies That Are Truly Color Blind," *Life: Special Issue*, 39.
3. *New York Times*, February 9, 1988, 38.
4. "Barriers," *Life: Special Issue*, 44.

CHAPTER EIGHT
1. "Special Report," *Newsweek*, March 7, 1988, 23.
2. "King," *Life: Special Issue*, 29.

RECOMMENDED
READING

Auletta, Ken. *The Underclass.* New York: Random House, 1982.

Belfage, Sally. *Freedom Summer.* New York: Viking, 1965.

Bennett, Lerone, Jr. *Before the Mayflower:* A History of Black America. New York: Penguin, 1984.

Fager, Charles. *Selma 1965.* Boston: Beacon Press, 1985.

Farmer, James. *Lay Bare the Heart: An Autobiography of the Civil Rights Movement.* New York: Arbor House, 1985.

Forman, James. *The Making of Black Revolutionaries.* New York: Macmillan, 1972.

Hamer, Fannie Lou. *To Praise Our Bridges: An Autobiography.* Jackson; KIPCO 1967.

Harding, Vincent. *There Is a River: The Black Struggle for Freedom in America.* New York: Harcourt Brace Jovanovich, 1981.

King, Martin Luther, Jr. *Why We Can't Wait.* New York: Harper & Row, 1964.

Kosof, Anna. *Jesse Jackson.* New York: Franklin Watts, 1987.

Lester, Julius. *All Is Well.* New York: William Morrow, 1976.

McCord, William. *Mississippi: The Long Hot Summer.* New York: Norton, 1965.

Meredith, James. *Three Years in Mississippi.* Bloomington, IN: Indiana University Press, 1966.

Monroe, Sylvester and Goodman, Peter. *Brothers, Black and Poor—A Story of Courage and Survival.* New York: A Newsweek Book / William Morrow, 1988.

Moody, Anne. *Coming of Age in Mississippi.* New York: Dial Press, 1968.

Oates, Stephen B. *Let the Trumpet Sound: The Life of Martin Luther King, Jr.* New York: Harper & Row, 1982.

Von Hoffman, Nicholas. *Mississippi Notebook.* New York: D. White, 1964.

Wilson, William Julius. *The Truly Disadvantaged.* Chicago: University of Chicago Press, 1987.

INDEX

Page numbers in *italics* refer to illustrations